CW00385758

REFLECTIONS

On Encouragement

REFLECTIONS ON ENCOURAGEMENT

Text Copyright © 1993 Warren W. Wiersbe
Extracted from WITH THE WORD, published in the USA by Thomas Nelson Inc., Nashville, Tn.

Photographs copyright © Noël Halsey

Published by Nelson Word Ltd 1993.

ISBN 0-85009-226-4   (Australia ISBN 1-86258-142-8)

All Scripture quotations are from The New Century Version, copyright © 1987, 1988, 1993 by Word Publishing. Used by permission.

Reproduced, printed and bound in Great Britain for Nelson Word Ltd., by Isis Press, Didcot, Oxon., England.

Photographs used in this book were taken at the following locations:

Front Cover Bay of Islands, New Zealand
Page   8/9   The Himalayas from Murray Hills, Pakistan
Page 10/11   Vancouver Island
Page 12/13   California Court
Page 14/15   Gardens in Surrey, England
Page 16/17   Douglas I.O.M.
Page 18/19   Bay of Islands, New Zealand
Page 20/21   Bay of Islands, New Zealand
Page 22/23   Gardens in Surrey, England
Page 24/25   Fiji
Page 26/27   Israel
Page 28/29   Israel

REFLECTIONS

On Encouragement

WORD PUBLISHING
Nelson Word Ltd
Milton Keynes, England

WORD AUSTRALIA
Kilsyth, Australia

WORD COMMUNICATIONS LTD
Vancouver, B.C., Canada

STRUIK CHRISTIAN BOOKS (PTY LTD)
Cape Town, South Africa

JOINT DISTRIBUTORS SINGAPORE —
ALBY COMMERCIAL ENTERPRISES PTE LTD
and
CAMPUS CRUSADE

CHRISTIAN MARKETING NEW ZEALAND LTD
Havelock North, New Zealand

JENSCO LTD
Hong Kong

SALVATION BOOK CENTRE
Malaysia

WARREN W. WIERSBE

WORD

BOOKS

PSALM 121

I look up to the hills,
  but where does my help come from?
My help comes from the LORD,
  who made heaven and earth.

He will not let you be defeated.
  He who guards you never sleeps.
He who guards Israel
  never rests or sleeps.
The LORD guards you.

The LORD is the shade that protects you
    from the sun.
The sun cannot hurt you during the day,
  and the moon cannot hurt you at night.

The LORD will protect you from all dangers;
  he will guard your life.
The LORD will guard you as you come
    and go,
  both now and for ever.

God is your Helper (1–2). The God who made the hills is the God who gives you help. He is a God of the hills and the valleys (1 Kings 20:23–30), and His help is available to all who will call upon Him.

God is your Keeper (3–8). The pilgrims travelled together for fellowship and safety because the roads were dangerous. The dangers in modern society are just as great, if not greater. But God goes *before you* (vv. 3–4) and stays awake to guide you and guard your path. He is *next to you* (v. 5) and *over you* (v. 6), and He will take you safely to Zion (vv. 7–8).

PSALM 16

Protect me, God,
  because I trust in you.

I said to the LORD, "You are my LORD.
  Every good thing I have comes from you."
As for the godly people in the world,
  they are the wonderful ones I enjoy.
But those who turn to idols
  will have much pain.
I will not offer blood to those idols
  or even speak their names.

No, the LORD is all I need.
  He takes care of me.
My share in life has been pleasant;
  my part has been beautiful.

I praise the LORD because he advises me.
  Even at night, I feel his leading.
I keep the LORD before me always.
  Because he is close by my side,
  I will not be hurt.

So I rejoice and am glad.
  Even my body has hope,
because you will not leave me in the grave.
  You will not let your holy one rot.
You will teach me how to live a holy life.
  Being with you will fill me with joy;
    at your right hand I will find pleasure for
      ever.

You have taken a giant step toward true Christian maturity when you can say to the Lord *and mean it*, "My goodness is nothing apart from You" (v. 2).

Good fellowship (3–4). God's people are not perfect, but we should delight in their fellowship and not in the fellowship of the world's crowd (2 Cor. 6:14–18). The world needs our witness, but we must take care not to start loving the world (1 John 2:15–17).

Good heritage (5–6). Not just God's gifts, but God Himself! What a joy it is to let God choose your inheritance for you instead of acting like the world and fighting for your "place in the sun".

Good counsel (7–8). God gives wisdom if you will ask Him (James 1:5). God teaches you in the darkness as well as in the light. These verses are summarised in Matthew 6:33.

Good hope (9–11). This passage is one of the few in the Old Testament dealing with resurrection. It refers to the resurrection of Christ (Acts 2:22–32), and that is what gives us our hope (1 Pet. 1:3).

PSALM 25
(verses 1–15)

LORD, I give myself to you;
  my God, I trust you.
Do not let me be disgraced;
  do not let my enemies laugh at me.
No one who trusts you will be disgraced,
  but those who sin without excuse will be
    disgraced.

LORD, tell me your ways.
  Show me how to live.
Guide me in your truth,
  and teach me, my God, my Saviour.
  I trust you all day long.
LORD, remember your mercy and love
  that you have shown since long ago.
Do not remember the sins
  and wrong things I did when I was young.
But remember to love me always
  because you are good, LORD.

The LORD is good and right;
  he points sinners to the right way.
He shows those who are humble how to do
    right,
  and he teaches them his ways.
All the LORD's ways are loving and true
  for those who follow the demands of his
    agreement.
For the sake of your name, LORD,
  forgive my many sins.
Are there those who respect the LORD?
  He will point them to the best way.
They will enjoy a good life,
  and their children will inherit the land.
The LORD tells his secrets to those who
    respect him;
  he tells them about his agreement.
My eyes are always looking to the LORD for
    help.
  He will keep me from any traps.

This Psalm is helpful when you are making decisions and seeking God's will. What kind of people does God guide?

Those who glorify Him (1–2). If you want His will for His glory, He will show you the right path. If you have selfish motives, He may let you have your way, and then you will regret it.

Those who wait (3). You are not wasting time when you wait on the Lord in prayer.

Those who ask (4–5). God wants to show you His ways, teach you His paths, and lead you in His truths. The Word of God and prayer always go together, to spend time in His Word. If you ask Him sincerely, He will answer you clearly.

Those who are clean (6–7, 16–22). Psalm 66:18 applies here, as does 1 John 1:9.

Those who submit (8–15). God does not guide rebels, but He joyfully leads those who fear Him and submit to His will (Ps. 32:8–9). Keep your eyes on the Lord and let Him have His way. He knows where He is going and what He is doing, so follow Him by faith.

The enemy was slandering David again, and he had no way to vindicate himself. Samuel Johnson called slander "the revenge of a coward", and it is. What should you do when people spread lies about you?

PSALM 86

(verses 11–17)

LORD, teach me what you want me to do,
 and I will live by your truth.
Teach me to respect you completely.
Lord, my God, I will praise you with all my
  heart,
 and I will honour your name for ever.
You have great love for me.
 You have saved me from death.

God, proud men are attacking me;
 a gang of cruel men is trying to kill me.
 They do not respect you.
But Lord, you are a God who shows mercy
  and is kind.
 You don't become angry quickly.
 You have great love and faithfulness.
Turn to me and have mercy.
 Give me, your servant, strength.
 Save me, the son of your female servant.
Show me a sign of your goodness.
 When my enemies look, they will be
  ashamed.
 You, LORD, have helped me and
  comforted me.

"Unite my heart" (11–13). A divided heart leads only to instability (James 1:5–8), because you cannot serve two masters (Matt. 6:22–24). With a single heart, fear the Lord, learn from the Lord, obey the Lord, and praise His name.

"Strengthen my hand" (14–17). David's strength and experience were inadequate to face the foe; he needed the strength of the Lord. David knew his theology (v. 15; Exod. 34:6; Neh. 9:17), and that helped him in his praying. The better you know God, the better you can approach Him with your needs.

PSALM 23

The Lord is my shepherd;
  I have everything I need.
He lets me rest in green pastures.
  He leads me to calm water.
He gives me new strength.
He leads me on paths that are right
  for the good of his name.
Even if I walk through a very dark valley,
  I will not be afraid,
because you are with me.
  Your rod and your staff comfort me.

You prepare a meal for me
  in front of my enemies.
You pour oil on my head;
  you fill my cup to overflowing.
Surely your goodness and love will be
    with me
  all my life,
and I will live in the house of the Lord
    for ever.

The Saviour who died for you also lives for you and cares for you, the way a shepherd cares for the sheep (John 10:1–18). If you can say, "The LORD is *my* Shepherd," you can also say, "I shall not want."

The Shepherd feeds us and leads us. Sheep must have grass and water to live, and the shepherd finds those essential elements for them. God meets the everyday needs of your life as you follow Him (Ps. 37:25; Phil. 4:18). Never worry!

If we wander, He seeks us and restores us, as He did with David, Jonah, and Peter. When we need to know which way to go, He shows us the right path and then goes before us to prepare the way. Even in the places of danger, we need not be afraid. (Note the change from "He" in vv. 1–3 to "You" in vv. 4–5). He is with you!

At the end of the dark valley, He has a special blessing for you: you drink of the refreshing water of life, and you receive the Spirit's anointing. The Shepherd is there to care for every hurt and heal every bruise.

One day, you will look back at your life and see that it was only "goodness and mercy," and that includes the valley experiences. If life is difficult today, just keep following the Shepherd; He will never lead you where He cannot care for you.

PSALM 26

LORD, defend me because I have lived
  an innocent life.
 I have trusted the LORD and never doubted.
LORD, try me and test me;
  look closely into my heart and mind.
I see your love,
  and I live by your truth.
I do not spend time with liars,
  nor do I make friends with those who hide
    their sin.
I hate the company of evil people,
  and I won't sit with the wicked.
I wash my hands to show I am innocent,
  and I come to your altar, LORD.
I raise my voice in praise
  and tell of all the miracles you have done.
LORD, I love the Temple where you live,
  where your glory is.

Do not kill me with those sinners
  or take my life with those murderers.
Evil is in their hands,
  and they do wrong for money.
But I have lived an innocent life,
  so save me and have mercy on me.

I stand in a safe place.
  LORD, I praise you in the great meeting.

Examine yourself (1–5). Is your life what it ought to be? Let God test your mind and heart (Ps. 139:23–24). In your walking, standing (v. 12), and sitting, are you keeping yourself clean (Ps. 1:1)? Sometimes God allows the enemy to attack us just to make us take time for a personal inventory.

Focus on the Lord (6–10). If you look at others, you will be upset, and if you look at yourself too long, you may get discouraged, *so focus your attention on the Lord.* Match your defects with His perfections and claim what you need from Him.

Keep serving the Lord (11–12). The enemy wants nothing better than to upset you and get you on a detour (Neh. 6:1–14). Continue to walk with the Lord and serve Him, come what may. Bless the Lord and don't complain. God will vindicate you in His time and in His own way.

"Look at others and be distressed; look at self and be depressed; look at Jesus and you will be blessed."

Anonymous

PSALM 97

The LORD is king. Let the earth rejoice;
  faraway lands should be glad.

Thick, dark clouds surround him.
  His kingdom is built on what is right and
    fair.
A fire goes before him
  and burns up his enemies all around.
His lightning lights up the world;
  when the people see it, they tremble.
The mountains melt like wax before the
    LORD,
  before the Lord of all the earth.
The heavens tell about his goodness,
  and all the people see his glory.

Those who worship idols should be ashamed;
  they boast about their gods.
  All the gods should worship the LORD.

When Jerusalem hears this, she is glad,
  and the towns of Judah rejoice.
  They are happy because of your
    judgements, LORD.
You are the LORD Most High over all the
    earth;
  you are supreme over all gods.

People who love the LORD hate evil.
  The LORD watches over those who
    follow him
  and frees them from the power of the
    wicked.
Light shines on those who do right;
  joy belongs to those who are honest.
Rejoice in the LORD, you who do right.
  Praise his holy name.

"The LORD reigns!" Not "the LORD *will reign*," but "the LORD reigns!" Right now! In another psalm the Lord declared, "I have set My King on My holy hill of Zion" (Ps. 2:6). We are children of the King.

Let the earth be glad (1–6). You may not see much righteousness and justice in the world today, but that does not mean God has been dethroned. For reasons we do not fully understand, God permits evil men to exploit the earth and its people, but one day He will come in power and glory and set things right.

Let Israel be glad (7–9). Israel has played the key part in God's gracious plan of salvation, witnessing the true God, passing the Bible on to us, and giving us the Saviour. The nation has suffered much, but one day her Messiah King will come in glory and fulfil the promises made to the patriarchs.

Let the righteous be glad (10–12). This group includes all of God's people, sinners declared righteous through faith in Jesus Christ (Rom. 3:21—4:8). They love the Lord and rejoice in the Lord. If you are yielded to the King, you have good reason to be glad, so joyfully tell the world, "The Lord reigns!"

"Rejoice, the Lord Is King!"

PSALM 117

All you nations, praise the LORD.
  All you people, praise him
because the LORD loves us very much,
  and his truth is everlasting.

This short psalm is about a big subject: helping all the nations to praise the Lord. God called Israel to be a blessing to all the nations of the world (Gen. 12:1–3), just as He has called His church to take the gospel to the whole world (Matt. 28:18–20).

The nations are worshipping false gods, so what do we tell them about the true God? That His mercy is great and His truth is enduring. What He does is merciful and what He says is dependable.

God blesses you so that you might be a blessing to others, not only the people you see every day but people you will never see until you get to heaven. Are you helping the peoples of the world learn about Jesus?

"The Spirit of Christ is the spirit of missions, and the nearer we get to Him the more intensely missionary we must become."
Henry Martyn

PSALM 119

(verses 129–136)

Your rules are wonderful.
   That is why I keep them.
Learning your words gives wisdom
   and understanding for the foolish.
I am nearly out of breath.
   I really want to learn your commands.
Look at me and have mercy on me
   as you do for those who love you.
Guide my steps as you promised;
   don't let any sin control me.
Save me from harmful people
   so I can obey your orders.
Show your kindness to me, your servant.
   Teach me your demands.
Tears stream from my eyes,
   because people do not obey your teachings.

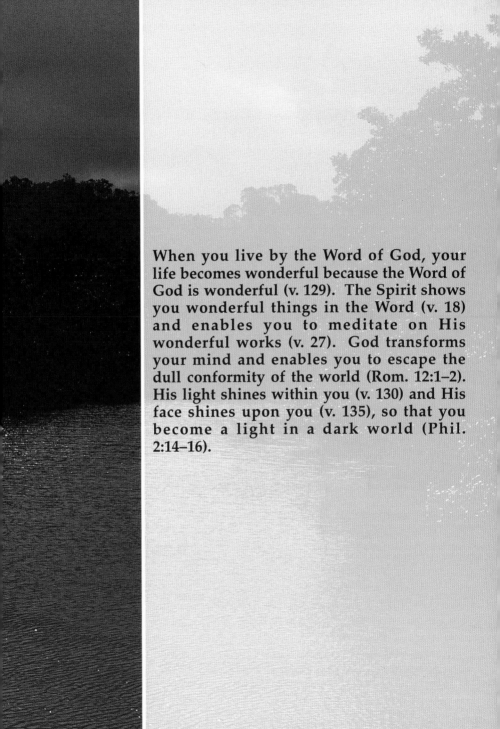

When you live by the Word of God, your life becomes wonderful because the Word of God is wonderful (v. 129). The Spirit shows you wonderful things in the Word (v. 18) and enables you to meditate on His wonderful works (v. 27). God transforms your mind and enables you to escape the dull conformity of the world (Rom. 12:1–2). His light shines within you (v. 130) and His face shines upon you (v. 135), so that you become a light in a dark world (Phil. 2:14–16).

PSALM 46

God is our protection and our strength.
  He always helps in times of trouble.
So we will not be afraid even if the earth
    shakes,
  or the mountains fall into the sea,
even if the oceans roar and foam,
  or the mountains shake at the raging sea.

There is a river that brings joy to the city
    of God,
  the holy place where God Most High lives.
God is in that city, and so it will not be
    shaken.
  God will help her at dawn.
Nations tremble and kingdoms shake.
  God shouts and the earth crumbles.

The Lord All-powerful is with us;
  the God of Jacob is our defender.

Come and see what the Lord has done,
  the amazing things he has done on the
    earth.
He stops wars everywhere on the earth.
  He breaks all bows and spears
  and burns up the chariots with fire.
God says, "Be quiet and know that I
    am God.
  I will be supreme over all the nations;
  I will be supreme in the earth."

The Lord All-powerful is with us;
  the God of Jacob is our defender.

This song was the inspiration for Martin Luther's "A Mighty Fortress Is Our God", and it can be an inspiration to you today.

When things are changing and threatening around you, focus your attention on God. He is with you (His presence); He is a refuge (His protection); He helps you (His power). Your world may be shaken with convulsions (vv. 2–3), but He has a river to give you peace (v. 4). You may be in the midst of battles, but He will end the war victoriously (vv. 8–9).

"Be still" (v. 10) means "take your hands off, relax". God knows what He is doing, and His timing is perfect (v. 5). When it is all over, He will be exalted (v. 10) and you will be blessed.

PSALM 90
(verses 1–2; 14–17)

Lord, you have been our home
    since the beginning.
Before the mountains were born
    and before you created the earth and the
        world,
you are God.
    You have always been, and you will
        always be.

Fill us with your love every morning.
    Then we will sing and rejoice all our
        lives.
We have seen years of trouble.
    Now give us as much joy as you gave us
        sorrow.
Show your servants the wonderful things
        you do;
    show your greatness to their children.
Lord our God, treat us well.
    Give us success in what we do;
    yes, give us success in what we do.

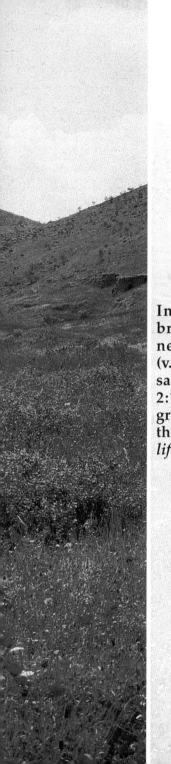

In the light of eternity (vv. 1–4), life is brief—no matter how long you live. You need God's help to use your days wisely (v. 12) and joyfully (vv. 14–15). There is real satisfaction in doing God's will (v. 14; 1 John 2:17), revealing God's glory (v. 16) and growing in God's beauty (v. 17). In spite of the burdens of life and the brevity of life, *life is worth living when you trust the Lord.*